Rudy the Rougarou
An Unknown Intruder

Written By
Daniel Reidmiller

Illustrated By
Alondra Paredes

For Our Grandchildren:

Stephen, Nathan, Dylan, Isabelle, Katie and Ethan

Special Thanks

First, I want to thank God for giving me the ability to capture the stories I've formed in my mind and put them down in print.

Second, I want to acknowledge and thank my wife, Marcia, for insisting we visit New Orleans back in 2009. I was not enthusiastic about going to New Orleans, but I found myself amazed and in love with the French Quarter.

Third, I want to thank tour guide extraordinaire, Jonathan Weiss, who owns Jonathan Weiss Tours, without whose passion for the history and legends about and surrounding New Orleans, I could not have imagined Rudy.

Finally, I want to thank Erin Rovin whose book, Little Laveau, inspired me to write a children's book based upon one of Louisiana's legendary creatures, the rougarou.

"Hi, my name is Rudy! Rudy the Rougarou. You pronounce it 'ROO-GAH-ROO,' and I live in a big swamp in Louisiana, called Manchac, and that's pronounced 'MAN-SHACK.' There are a lot of other swamps in Louisiana, but I live in this one. There are people who live in the swamps called Cajuns. Cajuns have been living in the swamps and on the bayous almost as long as rougarous have."

"Being a rougarou is a really special thing, because sometimes I'm a normal kid like you, but when there is a full moon, I don't have a choice and I change to look more like a wolf. Oh, I can make myself turn into a rougarou without the full moon, but I like being just a normal kid, too."

"My Paw Paw said that there are rougarous in places all around the world, but people call them werewolves. Here in Louisiana, we are called rougarous, which is Cajun for werewolf. I like to be called rougarou because it sounds a whole lot cooler than werewolf. So, to all my friends, I'm Rudy the ROUGAROOOO!"

"The swamp has a whole lot of water, but we also have lots and lots of trees, too. There are all kinds of animals in the swamp, like birds, frogs, catfish, and alligators. It is a fun place to live.

My best friend's name is Marshmallow. He's a raccoon and we do just about everything together. We play games together and we go fishing together, but usually we just seem to end up getting into trouble together. I'm going to go over to Marshmallow's house to see if he is at home."

So down the path Rudy went on his way to Marshmallow's house.

Rudy stopped along the way to join some frogs playing a game of 'Tag.' The frogs laughed and joked that Rudy was too slow to tag them, so Rudy concentrated really hard and changed into a rougarou. Rudy wasn't too slow anymore, and the frogs laughed louder because even though he was tagging them when it was his turn, he was also soaking wet from chasing them into the water.

Rudy thanked the frogs for playing tag with him, and went on his way.

Rudy came through the bushes near Marshmallow's house, walked up to his house, and saw the front door was open. Cautiously, Rudy peered through the open door.

"Hmmm, this is Marshmallow's house, but it doesn't look like he's home." Rudy said, "I wonder where he could be?"

Just as Rudy was ready to go back home, a tiny voice whispered to him from a tree across the path from Marshmallow's house.

"Hey! Rudy! Rudy! I'm over here!" the tiny voice said, "I'm up here in the tree. I've been hiding." Rudy looked up and saw two little eyes peeking at him though the leaves. It was Marshmallow!

"Hey, Marshmallow, what scared you up that tree?" asked Rudy. "I don't exactly know." Marshmallow said. "What do mean you don't know?" asked Rudy. "I don't know what it was," said Marshmallow as he scrambled down to the ground, "come on inside and I'll show you."

Rudy followed Marshmallow inside and sat down to hear Marshmallow's story.

Marshmallow poured two jars of sweet tea and set them on the table. Then he started

telling his story. "I went out this morning to pick some berries, and when I came home, I

found my door standing wide open."

Rudy could tell that Marshmallow was scared. "Did you lock the door?

What did you find?" asked Rudy. "No, I never lock my door, you know that." Marshmallow

said. "I found my cupboards open and my food was missing," he said with a gulp, "and there

are big claw marks on them! I got scared and ran up the tree across the path and hid there until

you came along."

Rudy saw the claw marks and his eyes got wide. "Wow!" he said, "You know,

Marshmallow, we should go talk to Paw Paw Doc and tell him about this."

Marshmallow nodded in agreement, "Yeah, let's get out of here!"

Rudy and Marshmallow followed the long path until they reached a big sign

that said, 'Keep Out,' they turned to go down the narrow path to Paw Paw Doc's cabin.

Standing on the porch was a tiny old man wearing a black top hat and was busily stirring a kettle.

"There's Paw Paw on the porch," said Rudy to Marshmallow, "He'll know what to do."

Marshmallow nodded to Rudy and said "Whatever he's cooking sure smells good!"

Rudy grinned at Marshmallow and said "You're always hungry."

Rudy and Marshmallow waved at Paw Paw Doc as they ran up to the porch. Paw Paw Doc looked at them and frowned. "Can't you read?" he asked, "The sign says 'Keep Out.'" Rudy chuckled and said, "Paw Paw we know that doesn't mean us!" Paw Paw Doc's frown turned into a smile and he laughed out loud. "You're right," Paw Paw Doc chuckled, "it doesn't mean you two."

Paw Paw Doc took a deep breath, narrowed his eyes at Rudy and Marshmallow and said "What can Paw Paw Doc do for you?"

Marshmallow started to reach toward Paw Paw's kettle and asked, "What are you cooking, Paw Paw?" Paw Paw turned and slapped Marshmallow's hand away from the kettle and said "Nothing that concerns you, swamp rat." Marshmallow said "Hey! I'm not a nutria, I'm a raccoon!" as his stomach grumbled, "I'm just hungry."

Paw Paw Doc chuckled because he like teasing the boys and Marshmallow was the easiest to tease. "Something was in my house and stole my food!" Marshmallow exclaimed. Paw Paw Doc looked concerned and said "Okie dokie, boys sit down and tell ol' Paw Paw Doc all about it."

After listening to Rudy and Marshmallow tell their story, Paw Paw Doc got up from his rocking chair and went inside his house. He was only gone for about a minute, then came back holding something in his hands. "Here you go, boys,"

Paw Paw Doc opened his hands "These are gris gris bags, they'll protect you from anything bad."

Rudy and Marshmallow took the gris gris bags and hung them around their necks.

"Thank you, Paw Paw," the boys said. "You're welcome, boys," Paw Paw said as he returned to

his kettle, "Now, ya'll get up out of here, ya heard? I got things I need to get done!"

Feeling safer after talking to Paw Paw Doc, the boys began their long walk back to

Marshmallow's house.

As the boys got closer to Marshmallow's house, they heard crying coming from bushes alongside the path. Rudy and Marshmallow stopped and carefully pushed the branches aside to see who was crying. They saw a furry creature with a very long snout sitting on the ground crying. Rudy knew whatever it was, it was very sad, so he nudged Marshmallow and they slowly moved toward the creature. The creature jumped when it saw Rudy and Marshmallow and threw its hands in the air, showing long sharp claws. Rudy reacted by turning into a rougarou and tried his best to look fierce, Marshmallow quickly scooted behind him.

"Stay back, don't hurt me!" the creature cried. Rudy was surprised and said "We're not going to hurt you, we saw your claws and we got scared." Then Rudy said "Hey! You have to be the one who ate all of Marshmallow's food! You left claw marks all over his cupboards."

The creature held his hands out in front of him and said, "I use these for digging up ants and termites. I eat other stuff, too but I really, really like ants. My name is Grover and I'm an anteater." He said, "I'm sorry for eating your food, but I came here to visit some friends and we went to go swimming, but I got hungry and went to look for ants. Before I knew it I was lost and couldn't find my way back to their house."

Rudy had calmed down and changed back into a little boy. Marshmallow smiled. "Well, it's nice to meet you, Grover. I'm Marshmallow and this is Rudy.

Come on back to my house with us and we'll see if we can find your friends."

Rudy took off his gris gris bag necklace and handed it to Grover, "Here, you can wear this. Paw Paw Doc says it good protection."

At Marshmallow's house, Rudy and Grover sat down at the kitchen table as Marshmallow disappeared into another room. Soon he came back with some things to eat.

"You missed this stuff," laughed Marshmallow. "At least we can have something to eat while we figure out how to find your friends." Marshmallow rubbed his stomach, "I'm starving!"

Grover placed a paw on Rudy's and Marshmallow's shoulders, smiled and said, "Thank you, so much. I know my friends are probably worried, but the nice thing is I have two new friends and that makes me happy." Rudy and

Marshmallow smiled, too, and they both nodded, "We're happy, too!"

Marshmallow and Rudy left Marshmallow's house to go and ask their swamp buddies if they knew where Grover's friends might live.

After talking to nearly every one of their swamp buddies, they finally happened across the frogs Rudy had been playing 'Tag' with and asked them if they knew who Grover's friends might be. The frogs sent out a message to other frogs and quickly got an answer. They discovered Grover's friends were a nutria family that live just around a couple bends in the bayou. Grover was excited, "Oh thank you! Thank you! Now I can go home!"

Everyone was happy. Rudy and Marshmallow took Grover to his friend's house. When they arrived, Grover's nutria friends, rushed to meet them. Grover was happy now and so were Rudy and Marshmallow.

Grover waved and said, "Thank you again, guys. I hope I see you both another time soon!" Rudy was smiling and nodding his head and Marshmallow said, "You're welcome! We hope we can see you soon, too!"

As the boys headed home, it started getting dark and the moon began to rise overhead. Marshmallow poked Rudy and asked, "Hey, you want to spend the night? We can…," but before Marshmallow could finish his sentence, Rudy chuckled and finished it for him "Roast Marshmallows, right?" Marshmallow grinned, "Well, they don't call me Marshmallow for nothing!" Rudy looked up at the full moon and smiled as he started to transform, saying "And I'm Rudy the *RougaROOOOOOO!*"

THE END

Thanks for reading 'Rudy the Rougarou – An Unknown Intruder.' Please join us in the continuing adventures of Rudy the Rougarou!